SAGITTARIUS

A GUIDED JOURNAL

Constance Stellas

ADAMS MEDIA
New York   London   Toronto   Sydney   New Delhi

Adams Media
An Imprint of Simon & Schuster, Inc.
100 Technology Center Drive
Stoughton, Massachusetts 02072

First Adams Media hardcover edition September 2022

ADAMS MEDIA and colophon are trademarks of Simon & Schuster.

For information about special discounts for bulk purchases, please contact Simon & Schuster Special Sales at 1-866-506-1949 or business@ simonandschuster.com.

The Simon & Schuster Speakers Bureau can bring authors to your live event. For more information or to book an event contact the Simon & Schuster Speakers Bureau at 1-866-248-3049 or visit our website at www.simonspeakers.com.

Interior design by Colleen Cunningham
Interior illustrations by Tess Armstrong
Interior images © Getty Images/Vikiss, Mara Fribus; Simon & Schuster, Inc.

Manufactured in China

10 9 8 7 6 5 4 3 2 1

ISBN 978-1-5072-1955-3

CONTENTS

INTRODUCTION

**Are you interested in how the stars may influence your char-
acteristics?** Wanting a little celestial insight into how you can
strengthen your relationships? Looking for guidance in using
your adventuresome and instinctive qualities? Guided journaling
can be a dialogue between your thoughts, feelings, and aspects
of your sign and element. By reflecting in an intentional way,
you can begin to understand yourself—and how you interact
with the world around you—better.

A fire sign, Sagittarians are fun-loving, blunt, and exuberant.
Journaling can help you develop the adventurous side of your
nature and tame more chaotic behaviors. Do you sometimes
make quick decisions you later regret? Does your love of a good
party sometimes get you into trouble? The prompts in this book
will allow you to have fun with no regrets by exploring your Sagittarian tendencies and what you may share with other fire signs.

Journaling can also help Sagittarius connect with and culti-
vate your wisdom. Your symbol, the centaur, is half animal and
half man. In mythology, centaurs were beasts given to riotous
living and fighting; they represented the unruly forces of nature.
However, the wisest teacher in ancient mythology was a centaur
named Chiron, who had integrated great learning and wisdom
into his wild self. Sagittarius's enthusiasm and good humor can

lead you into excess and hedonistic behavior, but as you mature, you might find that spiritual and scholarly pursuits begin to dominate. By reflecting on the prompts in this book, you'll gain a deeper understanding of how to balance your desire for enjoyment with making good choices.

When you write, you connect with your feelings, desires, and everything in between. And when prompts drive you to contemplate the wealth of astrological wisdom that each element and Sun sign offers, it can lead to surprising, creative insights. As a Sagittarius, you know you enjoy sharing good times, but you may not know that your exuberant joy can enhance fulfilling long-term relationships in work, marriage, and friendship. Or perhaps you had never considered the importance of visual, creative tools like vision boards as a fire sign. This book will help you explore yourself and your place among the stars.

HOW TO USE THIS BOOK

Welcome to your astrology journal! This guided journal is divided into three parts to help you explore your connections to the stars.

PART ONE

First, there are prompts about astrology in general, from how you feel about astrological wisdom to what you notice about your relationships with different signs and your experiences with reading horoscopes. The long and rich history of astrology can truly enhance your life and deepen your self-knowledge. Whatever strikes your fancy is a prompt to pursue! The purpose is not to master celestial knowledge but to turn your thoughts to the cosmos and reflect in an intentional way that may uncover some surprising insights.

PART TWO

The second part features prompts about your element. In astrology, there are four elements:

- Fire
- Earth
- Air
- Water

There are three zodiac signs in each element.

THE PASSIONATE FIRE SIGNS ARE:	ARIES	LEO	SAGITTARIUS

THE PRACTICAL EARTH SIGNS ARE:	TAURUS	VIRGO	CAPRICORN

THE COMMUNICATIVE AIR SIGNS ARE:	GEMINI	LIBRA	AQUARIUS

THE EMOTIONAL WATER SIGNS ARE:	CANCER	SCORPIO	PISCES

All members of the same element have an affinity; being with your elemental brothers or sisters can often feel comfortable because they speak your language. Understanding the characteristics of your element can give insight into good health practices and ways to relax and recharge, as well as how you might approach aspects of life such as work and relationships.

PART THREE

Finally, the third part of this journal concentrates on your Sun sign. This is the position of the sun when you were born. The Sun sign is a dominant feature in a person's entire chart. It reveals your:

- Psychological characteristics
- Health habits
- Relationship affinities
- Spiritual mission in this lifetime

Each Sun sign also has a ruling planet that gives the sign a certain kind of energy; a symbol that represents the characteristics of the sign's personality; and a modality that reveals whether that sign charges ahead in life, prefers the security of things remaining the same, or is open to the changes that come along. Consider these prompts intuitively. When something speaks to you and you think "Yes! That's me," reflect on the questions and any suggestions posed by the prompt. If you don't feel particularly drawn to a prompt, you may want to return to it later. If the information or questions in a prompt make you feel uncomfortable, consider whether there is something hidden or suppressed in your life that it awakens. Or you may use the page to explore why this doesn't fit you. True, not every aspect of the Sun sign will resonate with every person, so you may want to look at your full birth chart to help color the portrait of you that you create in this journal.

Astrology has become more and more popular, thanks to the ease of calculating birth charts online; the availability of daily, weekly, or monthly horoscopes delivered straight to your inbox; popular lists of famous people according to their Sun signs; and more. Ancient astrologers may have appreciated these options, *but* a computer is not a person, and the information that computer printouts offer is standard. Anyone born on the same day, time, year, and place as you would have the same astrology chart; however, people are individuals. There's a lot more to you than what is written about a Sun sign or astrological element. The beauty of this journal is that you can reflect on what astrology means to *you* and understand the nuances of your sign and element and how they do or don't relate to you as a unique person. Use this journal as your guide in exploring what the stars can teach you about yourself!

Astrology is the study of star and planetary patterns and what they mean for individuals and societies. Observing the regular motions of the sun, the moon, and other planets, ancient people became adept at interpreting what these celestial bodies and cycles meant. Today, there is a new renaissance in astrology, thanks to the Internet. Now anyone can find out the locations of the sun, the moon, Venus, and more at the time of their birth in just seconds, and subscribe to a service featuring daily, weekly, and monthly astrological forecasts. Consulting astrologers also offer star wisdom for health, business dealings, romance, spiritual development, and marriage.

In this part, you'll find thought-provoking prompts to guide you in reflecting on astrology in a more general context, rather than focusing on one specific sign or element. The sun, the moon, Mercury, Venus, Mars, Jupiter, Saturn, Uranus, Neptune, and Pluto: All of these celestial energies make up a natal chart and become a blueprint for gaining deeper self-knowledge and guiding your life. You can explore the astrological patterns in your family, track how different events like eclipses and equinoxes impact your mood and experiences, consider your beliefs on fate versus free will, and more. Enjoy this journey into the cosmos.

PART ONE

GETTING TO KNOW THE WORLD OF ASTROLOGY

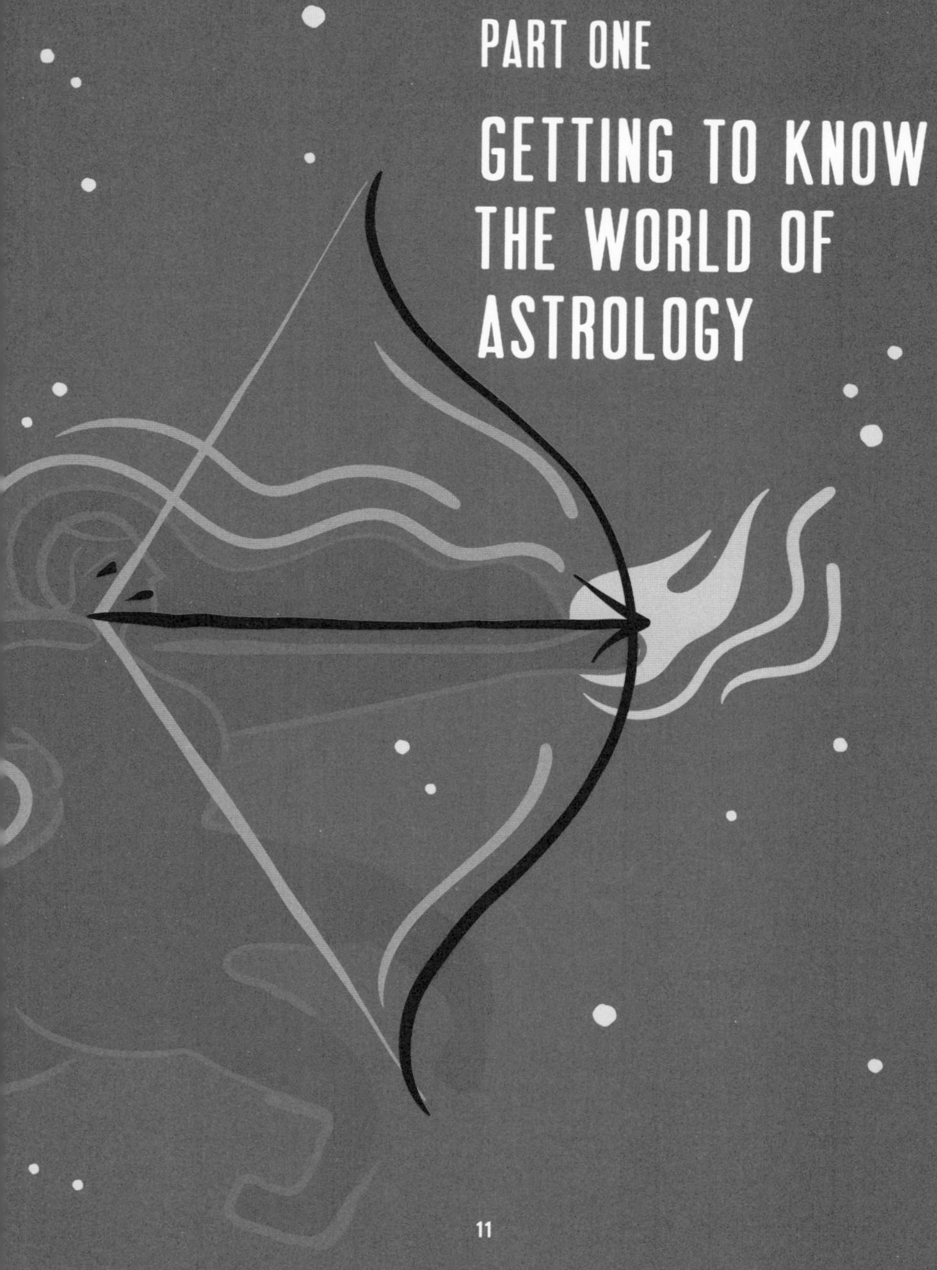

Imagine you are lying on the grass or a beach or sitting on a bench at night. You can see the stars, perhaps the moon. Depending on the time of year, you might even see Venus twinkling on the horizon or a distant red glow from Mars. Describe what you feel. Awe? Like you are part of the universe? Or like you are insignificant compared to the vast celestial sky? Maybe curious to know more about the heavens?

....

....

....

....

....

....

....

....

....

....

....

....

....

....

....

....

....

....

....

....

....

If you were an ancient navigator and only had the constellations and the moon with which to navigate your ship to get home, would you feel comforted by the regularity of the patterns in the night sky? Write about a time when you felt lost literally or emotionally. Did the moon or a twinkling star give you courage? Did you notice if the moon during that time was just a crescent or full? Or maybe it was somewhere in between?

Astrology has become more and more popular in recent years, thanks to the Internet! Do you believe that everything astrology says about your sign is true? Write about a positive experience you have had reading your horoscope. Did you follow the advice? What happened?

What charms you about astrology? What bothers or concerns you about it? Are you mindful of the monthly zodiac sign changes? Describe any feelings you have about how certain zodiac time periods affect you. For example, in spring, when the sun is in Aries, maybe you feel energized.

Are there certain signs with which you are more harmonious? Less harmonious? Write about your experiences.

A person's fate or destiny is a lifelong path. Describe how you feel when you read an astrological prediction for your future. Do you think it is good to know this information? Or better not to know? Do you use this information, keep it in mind, or ignore it?

Each zodiac sign is ruled by a planet or by the Sun or the Moon. Do you identify with Mercury, Venus, Mars, Jupiter, Saturn, Uranus, Neptune, Pluto, the Sun, or the Moon? Is it the planet your sign is ruled by? If not, describe your feelings about your own sign's planet. Do you think knowing more about your planet brings you insights into your personality or fortune?

....
....
....
....
....
....
....
....
....
....
....
....
....
....
....
....
....
....
....
....
....
....
....
....

The most famous—or infamous!—astrological event is Mercury Retrograde. This happens three times each year and means that Mercury appears to be moving backward in relation to the earth's orbit. It is common during these periods to experience electronic mishaps, communications going awry, and difficulties and delays in scheduling. Describe any Mercury Retrograde experiences you may have noticed. Were you forced to be more patient than usual?

If your Sun is in Gemini or Virgo, both signs ruled by Mercury, you may experience more personal confusion during Mercury in retrograde. Describe any personal confusion that you or your Gemini or Virgo friends experience at this time. Did you notice that you or they felt relief when Mercury was no longer retrograde?

....

....

....

....

....

....

....

....

....

....

....

....

....

....

....

....

....

....

....

....

....

....

....

....

The moon is our closest celestial neighbor, and its rhythms influence daily life. The monthly new moon marks the beginning of the moon's phases. At the new moon, people make wishes or set intentions with support from the moon's increasing energy as she waxes toward the full moon (the peak of lunar energy). Do you tend to notice the moon's phase, influence, or sign? Write about your relationship with and feeling toward this light.

Many astrologers believe that a person's chart can indicate past lives. What historical time period do you feel connected to? Who do you feel you might have been in a past life? What was your profession? Do you believe a past life can influence your present life? If so, how?

....
....
....
....
....
....
....
....
....
....
....
....
....
....
....
....
....
....
....
....
....
....
....
....
....
....

Each astrological sign is either masculine or feminine. This designation has nothing to do with gender or sexual orientation. The masculine signs radiate outwardly, and the feminine signs inwardly. Make a list of all the signs in your birth chart. Which energy dominates? Or perhaps they are equal? Do you feel these descriptions are true to your self-image?

In astrology, each sign has a symbol associated with it. Think about the symbol for your sign. Explore your feelings toward this symbol. Do any of its characteristics apply to you? You might write a story about yourself and what your symbol means to you. For example, as a Leo, are you more like a roaring lion or a purring cat?

As you will discover in this guided journey, there are four elements: fire, earth, air, and water. Each sign belongs to one element. Have you noticed that the signs of people you get along with have the same element as you do? Or a certain different element? Write about your experiences with people of the same and different elements.

Some people believe that following astrology curtails free will by forecasting the future. Do you believe this? Do you think it is possible that by knowing about your sign and using the stars as guides for the future you can make better choices in your life? Or do you feel controlled by what the stars say? Reflect on your feelings about free will and the stars.

Throughout the history of astrology, healers and physicians were required to study the positions of the planets in order to help their patients. They believed that the planetary energies could help or hinder healing the soul and body. What do you think about this idea? Can you implement any of your astrological insights into your health practices?

The position of the sun, the moon, and the ascendant are the three most important placements in a person's natal chart. If you know your birth time, you can easily determine these with the help of an app or astrology website. Explore your astrological trio and write down your feelings about these placements. Do you feel more connected to your moon or to your ascendant? Are there any patterns you notice, like the same element for each placement?

Eclipses were awesome phenomena for the ancients—and still have us in awe today! In a total solar eclipse, the sun's light is blocked by the moon, and the atmosphere darkens. In a lunar eclipse, the moon is blocked by the earth, and we cannot see this silvery orb. Most years have four eclipses. Do you pay attention to this heavenly event? Do you notice any patterns, either within yourself or in your surroundings during an eclipse? Research when the next eclipse will be, and record your feelings for the week leading up to the event.

How do you typically "use" astrology? Do you find it useful for self-understanding? Understanding other people? Exploring your friendships and/or partnerships? Do daily horoscopes guide your actions? Or do you see astrology as more of a guide for larger focuses in life? Write about an experience when an astrological tip helped you in some way.

....

....

....

....

....

....

....

....

....

....

....

....

....

....

....

....

....

....

....

....

....

....

....

....

....

Have you noticed that people in the same family often have the same signs? Or that other positions in their charts correspond? It's frequently the case! Take a look at your family's and extended family's signs, and reflect on the similarities and differences.

Saturn is the farthest planet you can see with the naked eye. It rules time, structure, and lessons of life. A major astrological transit is the Saturn Return, when Saturn returns to its natal chart position. This happens between ages twenty-eight and thirty. Where is Saturn in your chart? Have you experienced this return? Whether you have experienced your Saturn Return or not, write about your feelings toward the current path of your life, relationships, health, and spiritual development. If you have experienced your Saturn Return, how did your life look during these years?

Aside from your Saturn Return, another important transit (when a planet returns to its original position in your birth chart) is with the planet Jupiter. Jupiter is called the benefic of the zodiac. He helps us feel generous toward ourselves and others, is good for business, and can bring new areas of creativity into life. Jupiter returns to his birthplace every twelve years. Think about your birthday years at each twelfth year so far. Write about your feelings and activities in those years. Were the experiences positive? Expansive? Creative?

The solstices, summer and winter, occur at opposite signs: Cancer in the summer, and Capricorn in the winter. They mark the height of sunlight in summer and the depths of darkness in winter. How is your mood at these times? Describe how these essential astrological markers affect you.

Two major points in nature and the celestial calendar are the equinoxes: the fall equinox (Libra) and the spring equinox (Aries). These events mean there is equal daylight and darkness during that day. Do you have any particular feelings during these times of the year? Happy fall is coming after a hot summer? Or anticipating spring after a harsh winter? Write your feelings about the rhythm of nature and how it corresponds to your experience of the seasons. If you live in the southern hemisphere, the equinoxes are reversed.

If someone you know says, "I don't believe in astrology, it's rubbish," what do you say back? Write a dialogue between you and a skeptical person. What are your points of agreement? Of disagreement?

Have you ever noticed that some days feel lucky and positive and that during other days nothing seems to go right? It could be that the planetary pattern in the sky is not in harmony with your personal planets! Keep a record of good and bad days and the placements of the planets during each day. Reflect on any patterns. (You can find the daily position of the planets online.)

Throughout history, people have sought to understand the world around them. Today we have scientific equipment to inform us of the makeup of the universe, but ancient peoples could only observe the basic elements that they saw in their lives: fire, earth, air, and water. They associated each of these elements with an astrological sign and certain characteristics, and physicians used these characteristics to treat and heal their patients. The elements and their characteristics are:

FIRE (Aries, Leo, Sagittarius): Fire signs are known for their passionate energy and impetuosity. They often need to moderate their bursts of enthusiasm to prevent burnout.

EARTH (Taurus, Virgo, Capricorn): Earth signs are practical, cautious, and seek out security with a measured pace. Cultivating change and taking a few risks can enhance their lives, boost their health, and encourage flexibility.

AIR (Gemini, Libra, Aquarius): Air signs are changeable and mentally oriented; they enjoy living in creative possibilities and have highly sensitive nervous systems. Getting "down to earth" can help air signs move forward realistically.

WATER (Cancer, Scorpio, Pisces): Water is the element of feelings, and all water signs react to life emotionally. Calming their waves of emotion in order to see a situation clearly is a lifelong challenge for all water signs.

The more than two dozen prompts in this part of the book will give you a platform for understanding more about yourself and your nature based on your element.

PART TWO

GETTING TO KNOW YOUR ELEMENT

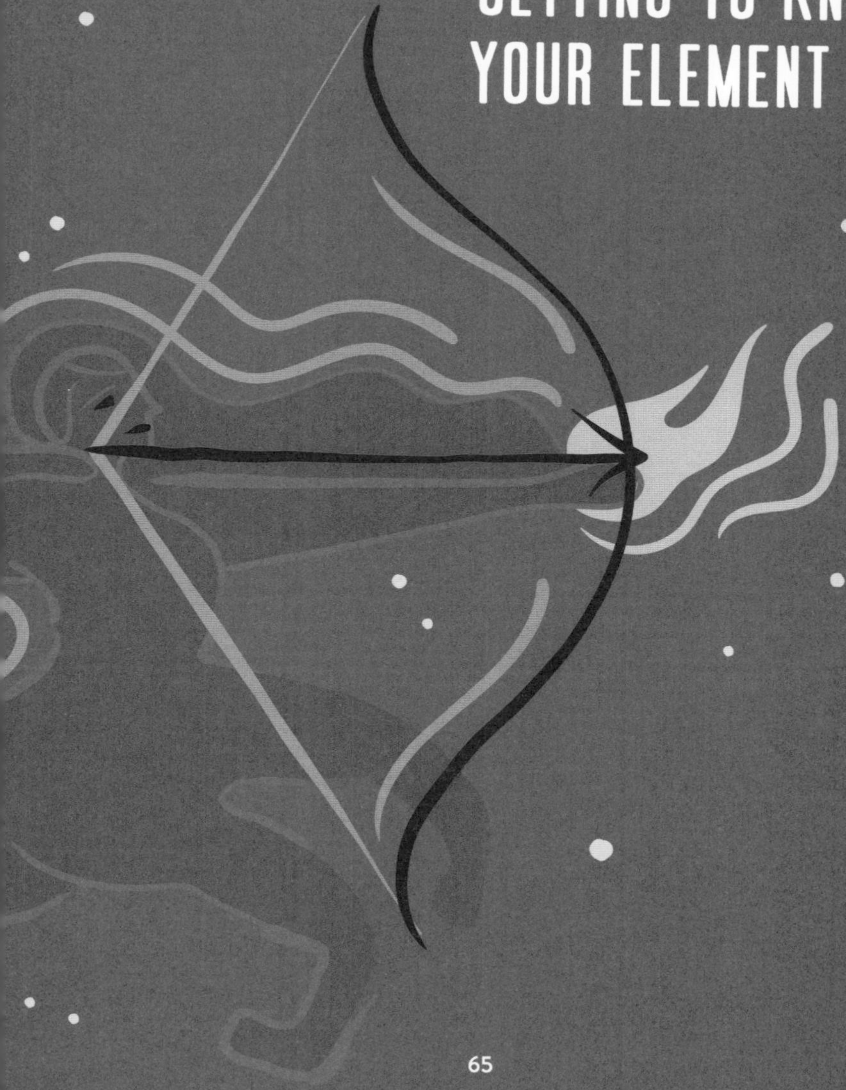

In astrology, fire is the first element of creation. Fire provides the spark that ignites passion and brings people together. Fire was also the foundation of communities: It invited people to gather for warmth and protection and to cook food. If you were a primitive human and discovered the warming power of fire, how would you feel? Now think about the current day and describe your favorite experiences with fire, such as campfires, candles, and so on.

One characteristic of all fire signs is their bursts of energy. Once you start, it is difficult to moderate your enthusiasm. Yet without a few rest stops, it can also be easy to burn out. Describe a time when you pushed your energy to the point of exhaustion. What clued you in that you were "running on empty"? How did you recharge your energy?

....
....
....
....
....
....
....
....
....
....
....
....
....
....
....
....
....
....
....
....
....
....
....

Mars, the Sun, and Jupiter are the planets that rule fire signs; each is a ball of energy and power. Mars symbolizes warlike fire; the Sun, health-giving exuberance; and Jupiter, spiritual and physical expansion. Do you feel compatible energies when you speak or interact with fellow fire signs (Aries, Leo, and Sagittarius)? Write down the adjectives that you feel describe your "clan."

....
....
....
....
....
....
....
....
....
....
....
....
....
....
....
....
....
....
....
....
....
....
....

In Greek mythology, Prometheus gave fire to mortals because he had such affection for people on Earth. He was punished for this deed, but civilization grew from his gift. What do you consider the greatest blessing of fire for humans? Write down your feelings about this essential element.

Fire can be beautiful, but it can also burn and destroy. Many weapons get their power from fire in one form or another. Write down your feelings about destructive firepower. How could this manifest itself in your life?

Fire signs are temperamental because their energy insists on burning freely. Describe a time when your anger was stoked and yielded positive results. Conversely, write about a time when you contained the blaze and benefited from moderation.

At the beginning of recorded history, fire brought hunters into communities and encouraged agriculture. Slowly, fire was used to cook food. Today, many fire signs become expert chefs. Think about whether or not you like to cook. What are your favorite tastes and recipes? Describe any important experiences you have had cooking for yourself and/or others.

Today, fire glows in fireplaces or decorates our homes in the form of candles. What is your favorite way to appreciate fire? Describe a personal experience with the glow of embers, a barbecue, or a candlelit room.

Enthusiasm is the lifeblood of all fire signs. Even if it seems like nothing is going on in your life, you will find something to be enthusiastic about. In fact, fire signs sometimes play a game with themselves and make the most ordinary chores dramatic, exciting, and interesting. Describe a time when you encouraged yourself by making a game of a tedious task.

Fire is the element of spirit and is used in rituals to purify and cleanse. Describe any purifying experiences or feelings you have had with fire. What did you do, and what were the results?

The element fire is fundamentally a creative force, and fire signs can use their fire power in unsuspecting ways. Fire people often have "hunches" about opportunities or relationships. When their powerful energy is kindled, they find lucky opportunities or connect with people who can help them. Write about any lucky hunches that led you to a positive conclusion.

Health is usually robust among fire signs. Describe your own health routine. If you do not feel robust and suffer from low energy, examine your emotional life and see if something is creating a firewall that is smothering your natural exuberance.

....
....
....
....
....
....
....
....
....
....
....
....
....
....
....
....
....
....
....
....
....
....
....
....

In relationships, marriage, or dating, fire people want adventure and experiences. Nice dinners with candlelight are fine, but a special experience with perhaps a bit of danger is really the way to keep your love life's fires burning. Write about the best adventure you and a fire partner had. How did it move your relationship forward?

....
....
....
....
....
....
....
....
....
....
....
....
....
....
....
....
....
....
....
....
....
....
....
....

Which element do you imagine is most compatible with fire signs? (Here's a clue: Fire needs air to burn.) Describe how you connect with air signs, then write about relationships you have with each of the other elements: water, fire, and earth.

....
....
....
....
....
....
....
....
....
....
....
....
....
....
....
....
....
....
....
....
....
....
....
....
....

Which element is opposite to the fire signs? (Here's a clue: Water puts fire out.) Write about a positive or negative connection or relationship with any of the water signs: Cancer, Scorpio, or Pisces.

In the general pace of life, fire signs move quickly. Do you walk quickly? Does it annoy you to be slowed down by people ambling along? If you are in a car, do you drive fast? Have you received speeding tickets? Describe your ideal pace.

Which astrological element do you think would make an ideal world leader: fire, earth, air, or water? Why? Describe your ideal leader.

A fever is the body's way of burning up illness and infection. Most fire signs run a higher temperature than normal, and their fevers can be higher than for other elements. Have you experienced this? What are your best remedies for fevers? Describe your experiences with fevers.

Enthusiastic spontaneity is a common impulse for all fire signs. In what ways is this part of your character? Write about the last time when, on impulse, you decided to do something fun. Were you alone or with a partner/friend? Describe your feelings about this adventure.

Intimacy and sex are prime ways that fire signs show their passion. They love to feel close and share their passions, and flirting is a good way to start. Describe a time when flirting led to a closer relationship. Then write down what you imagine an ideal passionate relationship would look and feel like.

....
....
....
....
....
....
....
....
....
....
....
....
....
....
....
....
....
....
....
....
....
....
....
....

A single flame is a particularly good image to focus on during meditation. The blue center or the yellow/red aura glowing outwardly can calm your feelings as you breathe deeply. In times of stress, see if meditating on a single candle flame can help you calm down and focus. Write about your experiences.

Red is the primary color associated with fire. It symbolizes bravery, courage, anger, and passion. Write down how you feel about the color red. Does it suit you to wear red clothes? If you imagine the color red, what do you feel?

Some alternative healers associate different sounds with elements. Laughter is the sound connected to the fire element. Describe the best joke you ever heard. Does it still make you laugh? Write about the qualities of your laughter and your loved ones' laughter.

Fire signs are creative. This guided journal is just one way to spark your creativity—jot down some other ways here. Write the ideas down without judgment; you don't need to act on each one. After a few days, review your list and decide which ideas to bring to fruition, then describe your experiences.

A nature hike is the best exercise for fire signs. You will feel free, move your limbs, and take in the amazing views. Write about the best experience you have had with nature hikes. How did you feel afterward?

Have you ever considered burning up the papers, letters, or written "evidence" that you keep from a worn-out relationship? Destruction by fire is final and can free up your energy for new experiences. Write about a time when you safely burned the record of a difficult relationship or situation. How did you feel afterward?

The twelve astrological signs we know today come from the twelve constellations arranged around the ecliptic of the sun's path. Astrologers observe these signs and interpret their effect on people and events. For example, an astrologer may note that as a Virgo, a person might be great at analysis but find it challenging to synthesize all the details. And a Scorpio may be drawn to jobs or a certain career where they can investigate people or subjects, but a corporate structure doesn't appeal to them. Through understanding your Sun sign, you have a unique window of insight into yourself and your life!

The prompts in this part will guide you through a deeper exploration of your Sun sign and the traits, relationship dynamics, and more that may be influenced by this sign. Reflect on how your career path may be impacted by your sign. Consider how a certain characteristic linked to your sign plays into how you handle conflict with friends. Through guided journaling, this part will help you get to know yourself better. Of course, there is much more to astrology than your personal Sun sign. If you are interested in knowing even more about your relationship with the cosmos, you can also look at the other signs in your birth chart, such as your ascendant sign. Or you may want to focus more deeply on general astrology, as well as your Sun sign and sign element, and revisit different prompts to see how your reflections may evolve. This is *your* astrological journey: Let it take you wherever you want to go!

PART THREE

GETTING TO KNOW YOUR SIGN

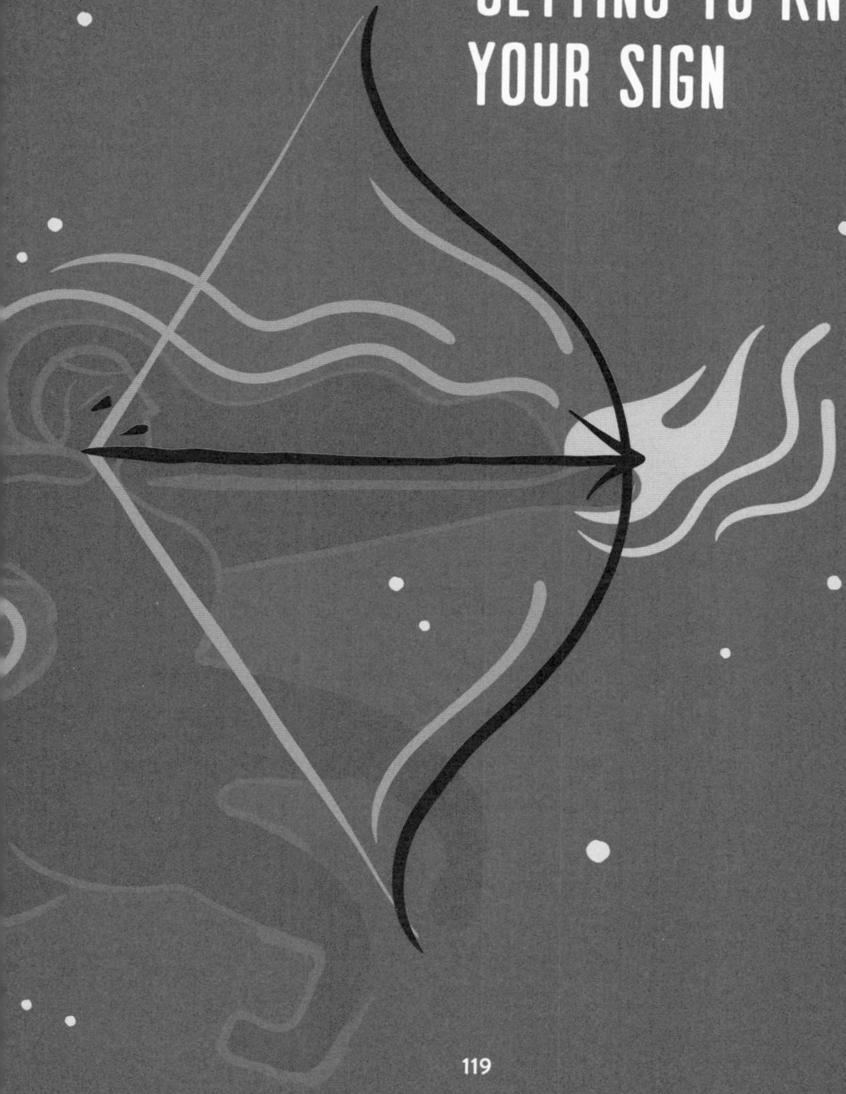

Sagittarius, a fire sign, has an interesting symbol—the centaur, which is a mythical half-man and half-horse figure. This symbol represents how Sagittarius needs to manage their dual nature: animal energy and appetites combined with civilized philosophical and spiritual aspirations. Which characteristic of Sagittarius do you identify the most with? Has this changed as you have matured?

....

....

....

....

....

....

....

....

....

....

....

....

....

....

....

....

....

....

....

....

....

....

....

Sagittarius is a mutable sign, which means it occurs during the change from one season to the next. People born in mutable signs are usually flexible and changeable. Write down the ways those characteristics resonate with your personality (or do not resonate with it). Then describe how you feel about autumn and winter—the seasons your sign is associated with.

....
....
....
....
....
....
....
....
....
....
....
....
....
....
....
....
....
....
....
....
....
....
....
....

Jupiter, the largest planet in our solar system, is your ruler. Jupiter was the chief Roman god, known for generosity, excess, and abundance. Being born under Sagittarius can give you a joyous outlook, luck, and good humor. In what ways does this description apply to you? Write about a time or times when your positive outlook helped you and others.

Each sign also has a shadow side. Sagittarius, being mutable and fiery, often has to deal with unstable relationships. For example, you may want to go off on your own adventure, while your partner prefers to stay closer to home. Write about a time when a meaningful relationship of yours ended because of your different viewpoints. Was there a big scene or just a fadeout? Describe any patterns you have noticed in your relationships.

Many Sagittarians are involved with a spiritual quest of some sort. Even if organized religion is not meaningful to you, an alternative spiritual discipline may be. What is your spiritual path? Describe any experiences you have had with your spirituality. Have they changed as you moved from childhood into adulthood?

Sagittarians have a talent for seeing the comedy in life and sharing it with their circle of friends. In what ways do you recognize this in yourself? What is the funniest situation you have ever found yourself in? Write about the experience and describe how it makes you feel to share laughter with others.

Though you are never intentionally malicious, Sagittarius calls it like it is, and is always truthful, if not tactful. Astrologers jokingly call this foot-in-mouth syndrome. Does this describe you? Write about a time when you said something true but inappropriate for the situation or person. Describe your feelings and other people's reactions. Would you do anything differently next time? Why or why not?

....

....

....

....

....

....

....

....

....

....

....

....

....

....

....

....

....

....

....

....

....

....

Sagittarius has fiery energy and is represented in the charts of many professional athletes. What is your favorite sport? Exercise such as Zumba, Buti Yoga, or cycling are natural practices for you—have you tried any of those? Write about your experiences with physical exercise. What changes do you want to make to your current fitness plan?

Routines bore Sagittarius. If a chore, game, class, or appointment is uninteresting, Sagittarius will most likely bolt. They don't mean to be irresponsible; it's just that there are too many other things to do that are fun! Write about a time when you left a boring event or situation. How did you feel when you left? What did you do instead?

Many Sagittarians love to travel. Visiting pilgrimage sites or holy places such as Jerusalem, Machu Picchu, or the pyramids might stimulate your philosophical and spiritual nature. Where is your favorite place to visit? Why? Where would you most like to go if you could travel anywhere in the world? Describe how that trip would unfold.

Which do you prefer: wide-open spaces in your home or a cozy, small place with lots of furniture and decor? Sagittarians are so energetic that they usually need space to move around, lest they knock over an end table that happened to get in the way. Describe your ideal home environment here.

....
....
....
....
....
....
....
....
....
....
....
....
....
....
....
....
....
....
....
....
....
....
....
....

Sagittarius wants to be comfortable and wear clothes that are outdoorsy, comfortable, and suggest adventure (bonus points for lots of pockets!). What is your favorite clothing style? Describe your current fashion sense. Now imagine that you are able to go shopping for a new wardrobe. What pieces do you choose and why? What colors are your favorite?

Sagittarius rules the hips and thighs. You may have well-developed muscles in these areas, as they are essential for walking, but it's still important to take good care of them. Stretching before you exercise will reduce strain and maintain flexibility. In what ways can you pay particular attention to loosening your hips and stretching your hamstrings and quadriceps? Describe your stretching routine in general. What improvements could you make?

Sagittarians can become restless when sitting still for long periods of time, whether for work or meditation. Try to avoid that by moving around! Choose a walking meditation or a workspace where you can stand. Write down your reaction to being confined in a small space or forced to sit still. How did you solve the problem?

Sagittarians can be a little blunt sometimes. But whenever there is a principle or value at stake, they have no hesitation in speaking their mind, without regard to political correctness or etiquette. Write about a time when you "told it like it is," even though it was unpopular. What made you feel passionate about the topic? What do you value about this part of your personality?

....
....
....
....
....
....
....
....
....
....
....
....
....
....
....
....
....
....
....
....
....
....
....

The Sagittarian symbol is a centaur—half horse and half man—
and you can certainly gallop through life with energy and speed.
However, remaining faithful to your commitments can sometimes
get left in the dust. Write about a time when you felt disappointed
that someone was not loyal to you. Then describe a time when you
did not honor a commitment. How did each of these experiences
feel?

Do you remember your dreams? If so, you might be able to recognize patterns or see future events in your life. Consider jotting notes down here to track your nighttime visions. You might even buy a dreamcatcher to hang over your bed. This is a carving or woven object that tribal people believe helps a person "catch" their dreams. In true Sagittarian form, go on an adventure to find an authentic one and write about your experience.

A mantra that Sagittarius would enjoy is "Keep Moving Forward." You can repeat this when you are feeling down or meditate on it daily for motivation. After a few days, write about what this mantra means for you. How have you used it? Did it help you through a difficult or painful experience?

Jupiter, Sagittarius's ruler, also rules good luck in the form of casinos, the lottery, or being in the right place at the right time. Write down examples of when your luck brought you good experiences. Then consider times when your luck was not fortunate. What happened? How did this experience make you feel? Do you consider yourself mostly lucky or unlucky?

Sagittarians sometimes find themselves going to excess in one way or another. Your exuberance, love of laughter, and energy can go beyond what's best for you sometimes. Write down an experience when your excitement led you to ignore practical considerations. How did you handle the fallout from your impractical faith that things will magically just work out? Write down what you learned from the experience. What would you do differently next time?

Sagittarians are extremely passionate about freedom and human rights. Write about which specific cause in this area means the most to you. Make a list of groups that are working to improve that situation and consider whether you can lend a hand. Write a description of how you would fix this problem if money were no object.

Music can boost your mood like nothing else. If you need a pick-me-up, play fellow Sagittarian Ludwig van Beethoven's *Ode to Joy*. This music epitomizes the free-flowing joy that is Sagittarius's greatest quality. Write down how listening to it makes you feel. Which event in your life could this song have provided the soundtrack to? Consider composing your own *Ode to Joy* in musical, artistic, or verbal form.

Sagittarius has such buoyant, breezy energy that the thought of traditional journaling may feel tiresome. If so, consider bullet journaling! Skip the long paragraphs and capture your thoughts in quick lists. If you want to expand on any of your thoughts or feelings, go ahead. Writing in any form helps clarify the mind and lift spirits as well, so don't feel bogged down by any one journaling style—choose whatever works for you.

Many Sagittarians enjoy the pure joy of comedy. Write down your favorite jokes or comedic situations and see if there is a pattern in the format or topic. What situations are the funniest to you? Do they involve relationships? Family members? Consider performing your funniest observations at a local comedy club.

Vision boards are a creative, pictorial way to "journal" your desires. Fire signs tend to be visual, so a vision board could help you see the future you want to create. Find images that represent your goals and arrange them on a board that you can hang up where you'll see it daily. After a week or two, write down how the vision board helps you focus your energy.

Sagittarians have a love of the outdoors and usually prefer the countryside to urban settings. Are you a city person or a country person? Which environment suits your lifestyle the most? Describe your ideal setting and your feelings when you are in the opposite environment.

....
....
....
....
....
....
....
....
....
....
....
....
....
....
....
....
....
....
....
....
....
....
....

ADDITIONAL RESOURCES

Websites and Other Digital Resources

www.alabe.com

www.astro.com

www.astrodienst.com

www.lunarium.co.uk

www.changingofthegods.com

App: Co-Star

Books

Astrology, Psychology and the Four Elements by Stephen Arroyo

The Astrology of Fate by Liz Greene

Sun Signs by Linda Goodman

Relationship Signs by Linda Goodman

If You Want to Write by Brenda Ueland

The Artist's Way by Julia Cameron

The Hidden Life of Trees by Peter Wohlleben

The Hidden Power of Everyday Things by Constance Stellas, Julie Gillentine, and Jonathan Sharp

Sex Signs by Constance Stellas

The Astrological Guide to Self-Care by Constance Stellas

How to Be an Astrologer by Constance Stellas

The Little Book of Self-Care by Constance Stellas

BIBLIOGRAPHY

Arroyo, Stephen. *Astrology, Psychology and the Four Elements.* Davis, CA: CRCS, 1975.

Arroyo, Stephen. *Relationships & Life Cycles.* Vancouver, WA: CRCS, 1979.

Donath, Emma Belle. *Have We Met Before?* Tempe, AZ: American Federation of Astrologers, 1982.

Forrest, Steven. *The Book of Neptune.* Borrego Springs, CA: Seven Paws, 2016.

Forrest, Steven. *The Book of Fire.* Borrego Springs, CA: Seven Paws, 2019.

Green, Jeffrey Wolf. *Pluto: The Evolutionary Journey of the Soul, Volume I.* St. Paul, MN: Llewellyn, 1985.

Green, Jeffrey Wolf. *Pluto: The Soul's Evolution Through Relationships, Volume II.* St. Paul, MN: Llewellyn, 1997.

Greene, Liz. *The Astrology of Fate.* York Beach, ME: Weiser, 1984.

Hickey, Isabel M. *Astrology: A Cosmic Science.* Sebastopol, CA: CRCS, 2011.

Oken, Alan. *Soul Centered Astrology.* New York: Bantam, 1990.

Sargent, Lois Haines. *How to Handle Your Human Relations.* Tempe, AZ: American Federation of Astrologers, 1958.

Tester, Jim. *A History of Western Astrology.* New York: Ballantine, 1987.

Yott, Donald H. *Astrology and Reincarnation.* York Beach, ME: Weiser, 1989.

DEDICATION

To all those seeking the wisdom in their stars.

ACKNOWLEDGMENTS

I would like to thank Karen Cooper and everyone at Adams Media who helped with this book. To Brendan O'Neill, Katie Corcoran Lytle, Laura Daly, Julia Jacques, Sarah Doughty, Jo-Anne Duhamel, Julia DeGraf, and everyone else who worked on the manuscripts. To Frank Rivera, Priscilla Yuen, Colleen Cunningham, and Tess Armstrong for their work on the book's cover and interior design. I appreciated your team spirit and eagerness to dive into the riches of astrology.

Unique ways to refresh and restore—personalized for your
ZODIAC SIGN!

PICK UP OR DOWNLOAD YOUR COPIES TODAY!